THE REAL CHRISTMAS BOOK

ISBN 978-1-4234-8261-1

7777 W. BLUEMOUND RD. P.O. BOX 13819 MILWAUKEE, WI 53213

Visit Hal Leonard Online at
www.halleonard.com

PREFACE

The Real Book is the answer to the fake book. It is an alternative to the plethora of poorly designed, illegible, inaccurate, badly edited volumes which abound on the market today. The Real Book is extremely accurate, neat, and is designed, above all, for practical use. Every effort has been made to make it enjoyable to perform. Here are some of the primary features:

1. FORMAT
   a. The book is professionally copied and meticulously checked for accuracy in melody, harmony, and rhythms.
   b. Form within each tune, including both phrases and larger sections, is clearly delineated and placed in obvious visual arrangement.
   c. All two-page tunes open to face one another.
   d. Many popular songs remain true to their original harmonies with little or no reharmonization. Jazz interpretations of other songs, including traditional Christmas carols, are also included.
   e. A variety of recordings and alternate editions were consulted to create the most accurate and user-friendly representations of these songs.

2. SOURCE REFERENCE
   a. The composer(s) of every tune is listed.
   b. Every song presented in The Real Book is now fully licensed for use.

THE REAL CHRISTMAS BOOK

ALMOST DAY

—Huddie Ledbetter

(MED.) All I Want For Christmas Is You

— Mariah Carey / Walter Afanasieff

ANGELS FROM THE REALMS OF GLORY

(MED. FAST)

— HENRY T. SMART / JAMES MONTGOMERY

1. An - gels from the realms of glo - ry, wing your flight o'er
2. Shep - herds in the field a - bid - ing, watch - ing o'er your
3., 4. See additional lyrics

all the earth. Ye who sang cre - a - tion's sto - ry,
flocks by night, God with man is now re - sid - ing;

now pro - claim Mes - si - ah's birth.
yon - der shines the_ in - fant light.

Come and wor - ship!

Come and wor - ship! Wor - ship Christ, the new - born King!

new - born King!

Additional Lyrics

3. Sages, leave your contemplations,
   Brighter visions beam afar;
   Seek the great Desire of Nations;
   Ye have seen His natal star.

4. Saints, before the altar bending,
   Watching long in hope and fear,
   Suddenly the Lord, descending,
   In His temple shall appear.

(MED.) ANGELS WE HAVE HEARD ON HIGH

—Traditional French Carol/James Chadwick

1. An-gels we have heard on high, sweet-ly sing-ing
2. Shep-herds, why this ju-bi-lee, why your joy-ous

3.,4. *See additional lyrics*

o'er the plains. And the moun-tains in re-ply,
strains pro-long? What the glad-some ti-dings be

ech-o-ing their joy-ous strains. } Glo —
which in-spire your heav'n-ly song?

— ri-a in ex-cel-sis De - o.

Glo — — — — ri-a

in ex-cel-sis De - o. FINE

Additional Lyrics

3. Come to Bethlehem and see
   Him whose birth the angels sing.
   Come, adore on bended knee
   Christ the Lord, the newborn King.

4. See within a manger laid
   Jesus, Lord of heaven and earth!
   Mary, Joseph, lend your aid,
   With us sing our Savior's birth.

(Med.) As Long As There's Christmas

— Rachel Portman / Don Black

Female: Don't look in-side___ a stock-ing. Don't look un-der___ the
tree. The one thing we're___ look-ing for is
some-thing we can't see.___ Male: Far more pre-cious___ than
sil-ver and more splen-did___ than gold,___ this is
some - thing to treas-ure,___ but it's some - thing we___ can't
hold. Both: As long as there's
Christ - mas, I tru - ly be - lieve Male: that hope is the

Auld Lang Syne

-Traditional Scottish Melody / Robert Burns

[TAKE 1ST ENDING ON SOLOS]

AWAY IN A MANGER

—Jonathan E. Spillman / John T. McFarland

(Med.)

G6 D9 G6 G7 Cmaj7 Gmaj7 D7#5

A - way in a___ man - ger, no crib for His bed, the
near me, Lord__ Je - sus, I ask Thee to stay close

E-7 D7 Gmaj7 B-7 E-7 A7 D7 Ab7b5

lit - tle Lord Je - sus lay down His sweet head. The
by me for - ev - er and love me I pray. Bless

G6 D9 G6 G7 Cmaj7 Gmaj7 D7#5

stars in the___ heav - ens looked down where He lay. The
all the dear___ chil - dren in Thy ten - der care, and

E-7 D7 Gmaj7 G7b9 C-6 D9sus4 D7 G6

lit - tle Lord Je - sus, a - sleep in the hay. The___
take us to heav - en to live with Thee there. A -

Dmaj7 B-7 F#-7 B7 E-7 A7 D6

cat - tle are low - ing, the poor ba - by wakes, but___
way in a man - ger, no crib for His bed, the___

Dmaj7 B-7 F#-7 B7 E-7 A7 D7sus4 Ab9#5

lit - tle Lord Je - sus, no cry - ing___ He___ makes. I
lit - tle Lord Je - sus lay down___ His___ sweet___ head. The

Gmaj7 D9 G6 G7 Cmaj7 Gmaj7 D7#5 E-7 D7

love Thee, Lord__ Je - sus, look down from the sky, and stay by my
stars in the___ heav - ens looked down where He lay. The lit - tle Lord

Gmaj7 G7b9 C-6 D9sus4 D7 1. G6 D7#5 2. G6

cra - dle to watch lul - la - by. Be hay.
Je - sus a - sleep in the

16

AWAY IN A MANGER

(SLOW)

—JAMES R. MURRAY / JOHN T. MCFARLAND

18

BABY, IT'S COLD OUTSIDE

—FRANK LOESSER

THE BOAR'S HEAD CAROL

(MED.)

Traditional English Carol

(Flowing) BRING A TORCH, JEANNETTE, ISABELLA

17th Century French Provencal Carol

BRAZILIAN SLEIGH BELLS

(BRIGHT SAMBA)

— PERCY FAITH

Burgundian Carol

—Oscar Brand

(MED.)

CAROL OF THE BELLS

Ukrainian Christmas Carol

CAROLING, CAROLING

—Alfred Burt/Wihla Hutson

THE CHIPMUNK SONG

— Ross Bagdasarian

(MED.)

CHRIST WAS BORN ON CHRISTMAS DAY

TRADITIONAL

C-H-R-I-S-T-M-A-S

(Med.)

— Eddy Arnold/Jenny Lou Carson

When I was but a young-ster, Christ-mas meant one thing: that I'd be get-ting lots of toys that day. I learned a whole lot dif-f'rent when moth-er sat me down and taught me to spell Christ-mas this way: "C" is for the Christ child born up-on this day. "H" for her-ald

CHRISTMAS IS A-COMIN'
(MAY GOD BLESS YOU)

-FRANK LUTHER

(Freely) Christmas Is The Time To Say I Love You

—Billy Squier

(Ballad) CHRISTMAS TIME IS HERE

—Vince Guaraldi / Lee Mendelson

Christ-mas time is here, hap-pi-ness and
Snow-flakes in the air, car-ols ev-'ry-

cheer. Fun for all that chil-dren call their
where. Old-en times and an-cient rhymes of

fa-v'rite time of year. share.
love and dreams to

Sleigh-bells in the air, beau-ty ev-'ry-where.

Yule-tide by the fire-side and joy-ful mem-'ries there.

Christ-mas time is here, we'll be draw-ing near.

Oh, that we could al-ways see such spir-it through the year.

Coventry Carol

Traditional English Melody / Robert Croo

(MED. SLOW)

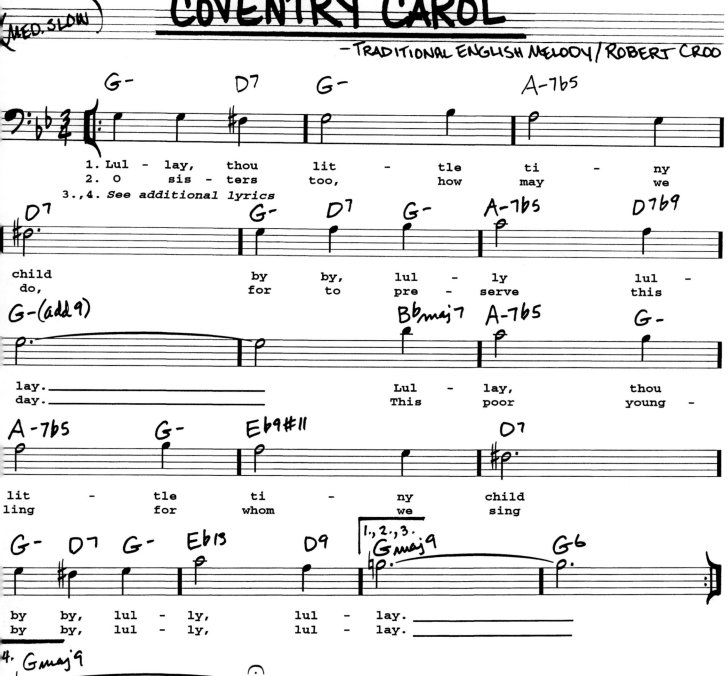

1. Lul - lay, thou lit - tle ti - ny child
2. O sis - ters too, how may we do,
3., 4. See additional lyrics

by by, lul - ly pre - serve lul - lay. this

Lul - lay, thou lit - tle ti - ny child by by, lul - ly, lul - lay.
This poor young - ling for whom we sing by by, lul - ly, lul - lay.

4. lay.

Additional Lyrics

3. Herod the king,
   In his raging,
   Charged he hath this day.
   His men of might,
   In his own sight,
   All young children to slay.

4. Then woe is me,
   Poor child for thee,
   And ever mourn and say,
   For thy parting
   Neither say nor sing
   By by, lully, lullay.

COLD DECEMBER NIGHTS

Michael McCary / Shawn Stockman

(MED. FAST) DANCE OF THE SUGAR PLUM FAIRY

-Pyotr Il'yich Tchaikovsky

(FAST) DECK THE HALL

TRADITIONAL WELSH CAROL

Deck the hall with boughs of hol - ly, fa, la, la, la, la, la,
See the blaz - ing yule be - fore us, fa, la, la, la, la, la,

la, la, la. 'Tis the sea - son to be jol - ly,
la, la, la. Strike the harp and join the cho - rus,

fa, la, la, la, la, la, la, la, la. Don we now our
fa, la, la, la, la, la, la, la, la. Fol - low me in

gay ap - par - el, fa, la, la, la, la, la, la, la, la.
mer - ry meas - ure, fa, la, la, la, la, la, la, la, la,

Troll the an - cient yule - tide car - ol, fa, la, la, la, la, la,
while I tell of yule - tide treas - ure, fa, la, la, la, la, la,

la, la, la. la, la, la.

DING DONG! MERRILY ON HIGH!

— FRENCH CAROL

(MED.)

Do You Hear What I Hear

-Noel Regney / Gloria Shayne

Additional Lyrics

3. Said the shepherd boy to the mighty king,
   "Do you know what I know?
   In your palace warm, mighty king,
   Do you know what I know?
   A Child, a Child shivers in the cold;
   Let us bring Him silver and gold,
   Let us bring Him silver and gold."

4. Said the king to the people ev'rywhere,
   "Listen to what I say!
   Pray for peace, people ev'rywhere,
   Listen to what I say!
   The Child, the Child, sleeping in the night,
   He will bring us goodness and light,
   He will bring us goodness and light."

Feliz Navidad

—Jose Feliciano

THE FIRST NOËL

(MED. SLOW)

— W. SANDYS' CHRISTMAS CAROLS / 17th CENTURY ENGLISH CAROL

Additional Lyrics

3. And by the light of that same star,
   Three wise men came from country far;
   To seek for a King was their intent,
   And to follow the star wherever it went.

4. This star drew nigh to the northwest,
   O'er Bethlehem it took its rest;
   And there it did both stop and stay,
   Right over the place where Jesus lay.

5. Then entered in those wise men three,
   Full reverently upon their knee,
   And offered there in His presence,
   Their gold, and myrrh, and frankincense.

THE FRIENDLY BEASTS

(SLOW)

Traditional English Carol

1. Je - sus, our broth - er, kind and good was hum - bly born in a sta - ble rude. And the friend - ly beasts a - round Him stood. Je - sus, our broth - er, kind and good.

2. "I," said the don - key shag - gy and brown, "I car - ried His moth - er up hill and down; I car - ried His moth - er to Beth - le - hem town." "I," said the don - key, shag - gy and brown.

Additional Lyrics

3. "I," said the cow all white and red,
"I gave Him my manger for His bed;
I gave Him my hay to pillow His head."
"I," said the cow all white and red.

4. "I," said the sheep with the curly horn,
"I gave Him my wool for His blanket warm;
He wore my coat on Christmas morn."
"I," said the sheep with the curly horn.

5. "I," said the dove from the rafters high,
"I cooed Him to sleep that He would not cry;
We cooed Him to sleep, my mate and I."
"I," said the dove from the rafters high.

6. Thus every beast by some good spell,
In the stable dark was glad to tell
Of the gift he gave Emanuel,
The gift he gave Emanuel.

(SLOW) FROM HEAVEN ABOVE TO EARTH I COME

GEISTLICHE LIEDER, 1539/MARTIN LUTHER

54

FROSTY THE SNOW MAN

— STEVE NELSON/JACK ROLLINS

(MED.)

A Cmaj7 · C7 · F6 · F#°7

Frost - y the snow man was a jol - ly hap - py soul,_
Frost - y the snow man knew the sun was hot that day,_

Cmaj7 · C7 · F6 · F#-7 · B7 · E-7 · A7

_ with a corn cob pipe and a but - ton nose_ and two
_ so he said, "Let's run and we'll have some fun_ now be -

D-7 · G7 · E-7 Eb7 Abmaj7 Db9#11 **B** Cmaj7

eyes made out of coal. Frost - y the
fore I melt a - way." Down to the

C7 · F6 · F#°7 · Cmaj7 · C7

snow man is a fair - y tale, they say._ He was
vil - lage, with a broom - stick in his hand,_ run - ning

F6 · F#-7 · B7 · E-7 · A7 · D-7 · G7 G7b9

made of snow but the chil - dren know_ how he came to life one
here and there all a - round the square,_ say - in', "Catch me if you

C6 · C7 · **C** F#-7b5 · F-7 · E-7 · A7b9

day. There must have been some mag - ic in that
can." He led them down the streets of town right

D-7 · G7 · Cmaj7 · C6 · Gmaj7

old silk hat they found. For when they placed it
to the traf - fic cop. And he on - ly paused a

Fum, Fum, Fum

Traditional Catalonian Carol

GESÙ BAMBINO
(THE INFANT JESUS)

(JAZZ WALTZ)

—PIETRO YON / FREDERICK H. MARTENS

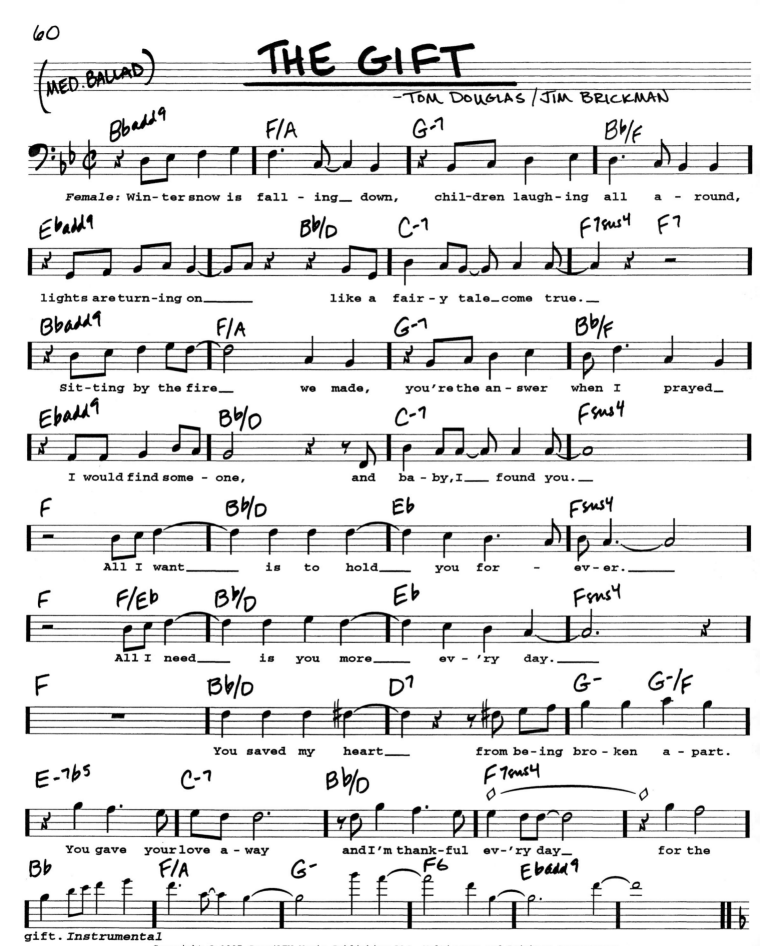

gift. Instrumental

(MED.) GOOD CHRISTIAN MEN, REJOICE

14TH CENTURY GERMAN MELODY / 14TH CENTURY LATIN TEXT TRANSLATED BY JOHN MASON NEALE

GOOD KING WENCESLAS

—PIAE CANTIONES / JOHN M. NEALE

(MED. FAST)

GREENWILLOW CHRISTMAS

-FRANK LOESSER

68

GRANDMA'S KILLER FRUITCAKE

— ELMO SHROPSHIRE / RITA ABRAMS

1. The hol-i-days were up - on us and things were go-in'
2., 3. *See additional lyrics*

fine, 'til the day I heard the door-bell and a

chill ran up my spine. I grabbed the wife and

chil-dren as the post-man wheeled it in. A

year-ly Christ-mas night-mare has just come back a-

gain. It was hard-er than the head of Un-cle Buck-y,

heav-y as a ser - mon of Preach - er Luck - y.   One's e-nough to give the whole

state   of Ken-tuck - y a great big bel-ly - ache.   It   was

dens-er than a drove   of   barn - yard tur - keys,   tough-er than a truck - load of

all - beef jerk - y.   Dri-er than a drought in   Al - bu - quer - que,

Grand - ma's kill-er fruit - cake.   2. Now   Grand - ma's kill-er fruit -
                                       3. It's

cake.

Additional Lyrics

2. Now I've had to swallow some marginal fare at our family feast.
   I even downed Aunt Dolly's possom pie just to keep the family peace.
   I winced at Wilma's gizzard mousse, but said it tasted fine,
   But that lethal weapon that Grandma bakes is where I draw the line.

3. It's early Christmas morning, the phone rings us awake.
   It's Grandma, Pa, she wants to know how we liked the cake.
   "Well, Grandma, I never… Uh, we couldn't… It was unbelievable, that's for sure!
   What's that you say? Oh, no, Grandma, Pul-leeez don't send us more!"

Grown-Up Christmas List

-David Foster/Linda Thompson-Jenner

(Ballad)

1. G C/G D/G B7/D# E-7 B-7 Cmaj7 A-7 D7sus4 D7
list. Instrumental
As
2. G C/G D/G G
list.
G7sus4 Cmaj7
What is_this il-lu-sion called? The in-no-cence of youth. May-be
E-7 A7 Dmaj7 F#7sus4 F#7
on-ly in__ our blind be-lief_can we ev-er find the truth.
Bmaj7 F#7 G#-7 D#-7 Emaj7 D#-7 C#-7 F#7sus4 F#7
Instrumental
Abmaj7 C-7/F F-7 Dbmaj7 Bb-7 Bb-7/Eb
No more lives_ torn__ a - part and wars would nev - er
C-7 F-7 F-7/Eb Dbmaj7 Eb7sus4
start and time would heal__ all hearts.
Abmaj7 C-7/F F-7 Dbmaj7 Bb-7 Bb-7/Eb
And ev - 'ry-one would have___ a friend and right would al - ways
C-7 F-7 F-7/Eb D-7b5 G7b9#5 C-7 F-7 Bb-7 Eb7sus4
win and love would nev - er end. This is___ my grown-up Christ-mas
C-7 F-7 D-7b5 Db9#11 C-7 F-7 Bb-7 Eb7 Abadd2 (F7sus4 F7)
list. This is my on-ly life-long_ wish. This is my grown-up Christ-mas list.

HALLELUJAH CHORUS

-George Frideric Handel

HAPPY CHRISTMAS, LITTLE FRIEND

Richard Rodgers/Oscar Hammerstein II

HAPPY HOLIDAY

—IRVING BERLIN

HAPPY HANUKKAH, MY FRIEND
(THE HANUKKAH SONG)

-Justin Wilde/Douglas Alan Konecky

HAPPY XMAS
(WAR IS OVER)

-John Lennon/Yoko Ono

(Med.) HARK! THE HERALD ANGELS SING

—Felix Mendelssohn-Bartholdy/William H.Cummings/Charles Wesley/George Whitefield

HE

Jack Richards / Richard Mullen

[TAKE 1st ENDING FOR SOLOS]

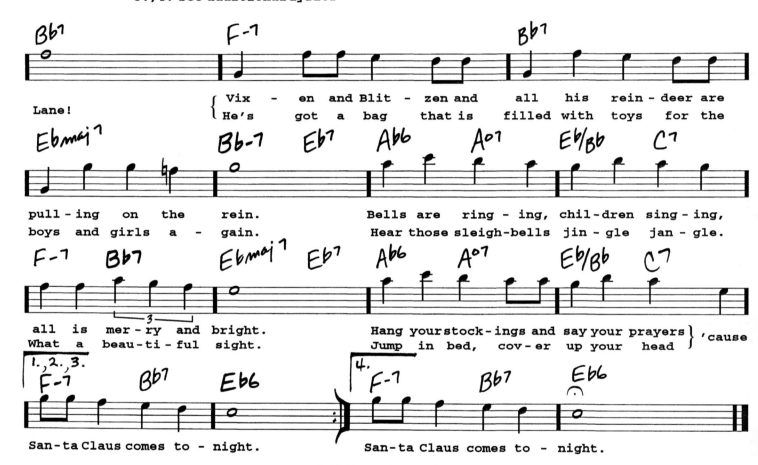

Additional Lyrics

3. Here comes Santa Claus! Here comes Santa Claus
   Right down Santa Claus Lane!
   He doesn't care if you're rich or poor,
   For he loves you just the same.
   Santa knows that we're God's Children;
   That makes everything right.
   Fill your hearts with Christmas cheer
   'Cause Santa Claus comes tonight.

4. Here comes Santa Claus! Here comes Santa Claus
   Right down Santa Claus Lane!
   He'll come around when the chimes ring out,
   Then it's Christmas morn again.
   Peace on earth will come to all if
   We just follow the light.
   Let's give thanks to the Lord above
   'Cause Santa Claus comes tonight.

THE HOLLY AND THE IVY

(SLOW)

—18th Century English Carol

A HOLLY JOLLY CHRISTMAS

-Johnny Marks

(There's No Place Like)
HOME FOR THE HOLIDAYS
— Robert Allen / Al Stillman

(Med.)

Oh, there's no place like home for the hol - i - days _____ 'cause no mat - ter how far a - way you roam. _____

When you pine for the
If you pine want to be

sun - shine of a friend - ly gaze, _____
hap - py in a mil - lion ways, _____

for the hol - i - days you can't beat home, sweet home.

I met a man who lives in Ten - nes - see and
A home that knows your joy and laugh - ter filled with

I Saw Mommy Kissing Santa Claus

—Tommie Connor

94

I Wonder As I Wander

(MED.)

-John Jacob Niles

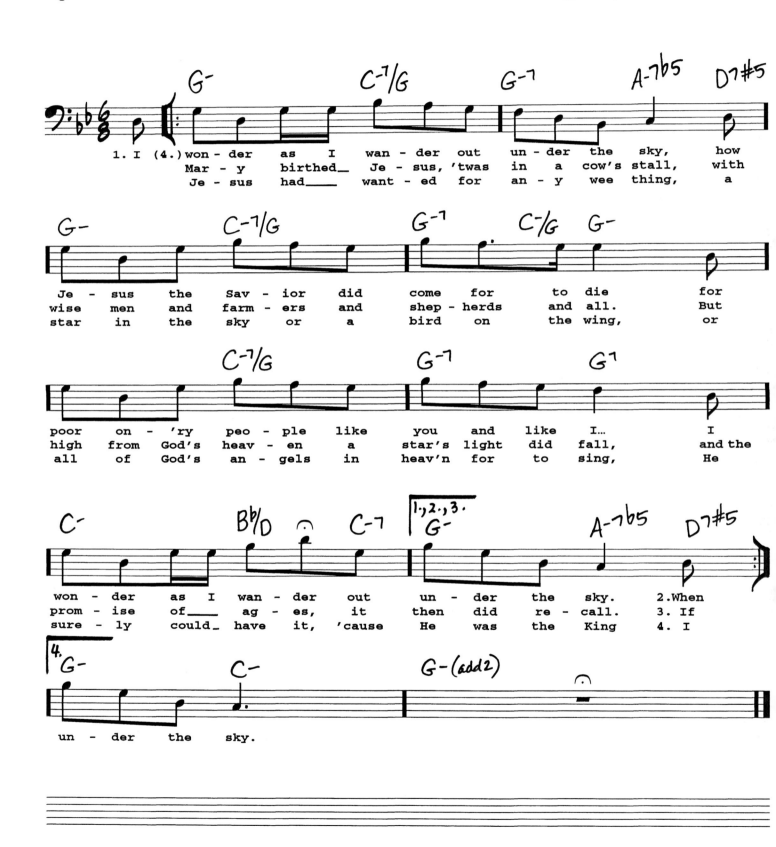

I've Got My Love To Keep Me Warm

-Irving Berlin

I'LL BE HOME FOR CHRISTMAS

— Kim Gannon / Walter Kent

(Med) It Came Upon The Midnight Clear

-Traditional English Melody/Arthur Sullivan/Edmund H. Sears

It's A Big Wide Wonderful World

-John Rox

(Med. Waltz)

It's a big wide won-der-ful world you live in.
brave new star-span-gled sky a-bove you.

When you're in love, you're a mas-ter of all you sur-vey; you're a gay San-ta Claus. There's a
When you're in love, you're a he-ro, a Ne-ro, A-pol-lo, the Wiz-ard of Oz. You've a

king-dom, pow-er and glo-ry, the old, old, old-est of sto-ries is new, true. You've built your
Rome in just one day. Life is

mys-tic, a mid-sum-mer's night, you live in, a Turk-ish De-light, you're in heav-en. It's
swell when you're real-ly in love.

IT MUST HAVE BEEN THE MISTLETOE
(OUR FIRST CHRISTMAS)

-Justin Wilde / Doug Konecky

(MED.)

Fmaj7 It must have been the mis-tle-toe, **A-7** the la-zy fire, the fall-ing snow, the

Bbmaj7 mag-ic in the frost-y air, **C9sus4** that feel - ing ev-'ry-where. It

Fmaj7 must have been the pret-ty lights **C-7** that glis - tened **F7** in the si-lent night, or

Bbmaj7 may-be just **G-7** the stars so bright **C9sus4** that shined a - bove you. **Bbmaj7** Our first

Fmaj7 Christ - mas, **D-7** **G-7** more than we'd been dream - ing **C7** of. **Fmaj7**

Bb-7 Old **Eb7** Saint **C-7** Nich - **F-7** 'las had his **Bb7sus4** fin-gers crossed, **Bb7** that

C9sus4 we would fall in love. **C9** It could have been **Fmaj7** the hol-i-day, the

A-7 mid-night ride up-on a sleigh, **Bbmaj7** the coun-try-side all dressed in white, that

C9sus4 cra - zy snow - ball fight. **Fmaj7** It could have been the stee-ple bell that

© Copyright 1979 Songcastle Music (ASCAP) and Cat's Whiskers Music (ASCAP)/both admin. by ICG.

It's Beginning To Look Like Christmas

-Meredith Willson

It's be - gin-ning to look a lot like Christ - mas, ev - 'ry-where you go.

Take a look in the five and ten,
There's a tree in the grand ho - tel,

glis-ten-ing once a - gain, with can - dy canes and sil - ver lanes a -
one in the park, as well, the stur - dy kind that does - n't mind the

glow._____ It's be - gin-ning to look a lot like
snow._____ It's be - gin-ning to look a lot like

Christ - mas, toys in ev - 'ry store. But the
Christ - mas, soon the bells will start. And the

pret - ti - est sight to see is the hol - ly that will be on your
thing that will make them ring is the car - ol that you sing right with -

own in   front your   door._____ A pair of

hop-a-long boots and a pis-tol that shoots is the wish of Bar-ney and Ben.

Dolls that will talk and will go for a walk is the hope of Jan-ice and Jen. And

Mom and Dad can hard-ly wait for school to start a-gain. It's be -

heart.

104

It's Christmas In New York

-Billy Butt

Church-bells are ring-ing, ____ choirs ____ are
Rest-'rant signs sway-ing, ____ blue skies are

sing-ing, ____ joy they are bring-ing, ____
gray-ing, ____ ev-'ry-one's say-ing, ____

it's Christ-mas in New York. Street-lights are
it's Christ-mas in New York. Sky-scrap-ers

pleas-ing, ____ snow-flakes are teas-ing, ____
gleam-ing, ____ Broad-way lights beam-ing, ____

Cen-tral Park's freez-ing, ____ it's Christ-mas in New
chil-dren are dream-ing, ____ it's Christ-mas in New

York. The stars ____ in the heav-ens are
York. The lights ____ on the Christ-mas tree

so ____ bright, ____ they tell ____
are ____ fine, ____ the sights ____

of a ba-by that was born ____ on this night.
of the shop-ping sprees, the gifts, ____ yours and mine.

SOLOS A A B A

It's Just Another New Year's Eve

—Barry Manilow/Marty Panzer

JESU, JOY OF MAN'S DESIRING

Johann Sebastian Bach/Robert Bridges

Jingle, Jingle, Jingle

-Johnny Marks

June In January

(Ballad)

— Leo Robin / Ralph Rainger

It's June in Jan-u-ar-y be-cause I'm in love;
snow is just white blos-soms that fall from a-bove,

it al-ways is spring in my heart, with you in my arms.____ The
and here is the rea-son, my dear: your

mag-i-cal charms.____ The night is cold,

the trees are bare, but I can feel the scent of

ros-es in the air. It's June in Jan-u-ar-y

be-cause I'm in love, but on-ly be-cause I'm in love with

you.____ FINE (It's)

Last Christmas

George Michael

120

THE LAST MONTH OF THE YEAR
(WHAT MONTH WAS JESUS BORN IN?)

-Vera Hall / Ruby Pickens Tartt / Alan Lomax

(Med.) LET'S HAVE AN OLD FASHIONED CHRISTMAS

-Joe Solomon / Larry Conley

Let's have an old fash-ioned Christ - mas;

dress up an old fash-ioned tree.

Let's make the spir-it of Auld Lang Syne the

same as it used to be.

Hearts will be light as a feath - er

af - ter some old fash-ioned cheer. So let's

all be good fel-lows to-geth - er; let's have an

old fash-ioned Christ-mas this year.

© 1939 (Renewed) EDWIN H. MORRIS & COMPANY, A Division of MPL Music Publishing, Inc.

126

(BALLAD)

LOST IN THE STARS

—Kurt Weill/Maxwell Anderson

132

134

(Freely) MERRY CHRISTMAS, DARLING
-Richard Carpenter/Frank Pooler

Greet-ing cards have all been sent, the Christ-mas rush is through, but I still have one wish to make, a spe-cial one for you:

(SLOWLY) Mer - ry Christ - mas, dar - ling. We're a - part, that's true; but I can dream and in my dreams, I'm Christ - mas-ing with you.

Hol - i - days are joy - ful, there's al-ways some - thing new. But ev - 'ry day's a

MERRY, MERRY CHRISTMAS, BABY

Margo Sylvia / Gilbert Lopez

MED. SLOW
50'S ROCK

Mer - ry, mer - ry Christ - mas, ba - by.

Al-though you're with some - bod-y new,

thought I'd send a card to say that I wish this hol-i-

day would find me be - side you.

Mer - ry, mer - ry Christ - mas, ba - by,

and a hap - py New Year too.

It was Christ - mas Eve we met, a hol-i-day I can't for-

140

A MERRY, MERRY CHRISTMAS TO YOU
(MED. FAST)

-JOHNNY MARKS

142

Mister Santa

—Pat Ballard

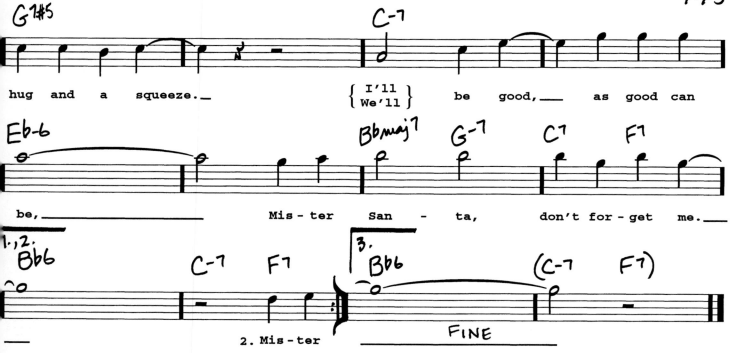

Additional Lyrics

2. Mister Santa, dear old Saint Nick,
   Be awful careful and please don't get sick.
   Put on your coat when breezes are blowin'
   And when you cross the street look where you're goin'.
   Santa, we (I) love you so,
   We (I) hope you never get lost in the snow.
   Take your time when you unpack,
   Mister Santa, don't hurry back.

3. Mister Santa, we've been so good,
   We've washed the dishes and done what we should.
   Made up the beds and scrubbed up our toesies,
   We've used a Kleenex when we've blown our nosesies.
   Santa, look at our ears, they're clean as whistles,
   We're sharper than shears.
   Now we've put you on the spot,
   Mister Santa, bring us a lot.

144

(FAST) THE MOST WONDERFUL DAY OF THE YEAR

-JOHNNY MARKS

Cmaj7 A7 D-7 G7

A pack-ful of toys means a sack-ful of joys for

Cmaj7 A7#5 D7 G7 C6

mil-lions of girls and for mil-lions of boys when Christ-mas

Eb°7 E-7 A7b9 D-7 G7

Day is here.____ The most won-der-ful day of the

Cmaj7 D-7 G7 Cmaj7 A7

year!____ { A Jack in the box waits for
{ It won't seem like Christ-mas 'til

D-7 G7 Cmaj7 A7#5

chil-dren to shout, "Wake up, don't you know that it's
Dad gets his tie, "It's just what I want-ed" is

D7 G7 C6 Eb°7

time to come out!"} When Christ-mas Day is
his year-ly cry! }

E-7 A7b9 D-7 G7

here,____ the most won-der-ful day of the

The Most Wonderful Time Of The Year

(MED. UP WALTZ)

—EDDIE POLA / GEORGE WYLE

B-7 E7 E-7
sea - son of all.
A7 Dmaj7 D#°7
There'll be par - ties for host - ing, marsh -
C#-7 F#-7 B-7
mal - lows for toast - ing and car - ol - ing
E7 Amaj7 A6
out in the snow. There'll be
D-7 G7 Cmaj7
scar - y ghost sto - ries and tales of the
Fmaj7 B-7b5
glo - ries of Christ - mas - es long, long a -
E7sus4 E7 D.S. AL
go. It's the
C#-7 F#-7 B-7 E7
most won - der - ful time of the
A6 (F#-7 B-7 E7)
year.

MY FAVORITE THINGS

— Richard Rodgers/ Oscar Hammerstein II

D.C. FOR SOLOS

NOËL! NOËL!

FRENCH-ENGLISH CAROL

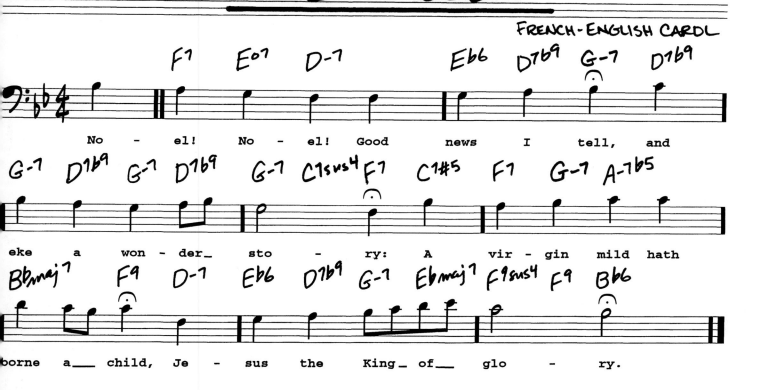

No - el! No - el! Good news I tell, and

eke a won-der_ sto - ry: A vir - gin mild hath

borne a__ child, Je - sus the King_ of__ glo - ry.

152

(Med.) THE NIGHT BEFORE CHRISTMAS SONG

—Johnny Marks/Lyrics Adapted by Johnny Marks from Clement Moore's Poem

153

154

melody x2

O Christmas Tree

—Traditional German Carol

(MED.)

O COME, ALL YE FAITHFUL
(ADESTE FIDELES)

(MED.)

-JOHN FRANCIS WADE/LATIN WORDS TRANSLATED BY FREDERICK OAKELEY

158

O Come, O Come Immanuel

(Ballad) O Little Town of Bethlehem

— Lewis H. Redner / Phillips Brooks

O HOLY NIGHT

-ADOLPHE ADAM / FRENCH WORDS BY PLACIDE CAPPEAU / ENGLISH WORDS BY
JOHN S. DWIGHT

(MED.)

162

PARADE OF THE WOODEN SOLDIERS

-Leon Jessel / Ballard MacDonald

PRETTY PAPER

— WILLIE NELSON

hop-ing_____ that you won't pass him by.

Should you stop; bet-ter not, much too

bus-y.__ You're__ in a hur-ry,_____ my, how time____ does

fly. In the dis-tance,_____ the ring-ing of

laugh-ter,_____ and in the midst of the laugh-ter_____ he

cries._____ Pret-ty

blue._____

168

Rockin' Around The Christmas Tree

(Med. Shuffle)

—Johnny Marks

Rock-in' a-round the Christ-mas tree at the Christ-mas par-ty hop.
Rock-in' a-round the Christ-mas tree, let the Christ-mas spir-it ring.

Mis-tle-toe hung where you can see ev-'ry
Lat-er we'll have where some pump-kin pie and we'll

1.
cou-ple tries to stop.

2.
do some car-ol-ing.

You will get a sen-ti-men-tal feel-ing when you hear

voic-es sing-ing, "Let's be jol-ly, deck the halls with boughs of hol-ly."

Rock-in' a-round the Christ-mas tree, have a hap-py hol-i-day.

AFTER SOLOS, D.C. AL ⊕
(TAKE REPEAT)

Ev-'ry-one danc-ing mer-ri-ly in the new old fash-ioned way.

new old fash-ioned way.

RUDOLPH THE RED-NOSED REINDEER

—Johnny Marks

Santa Baby

Joan Javits/Phil Springer/Tony Springer

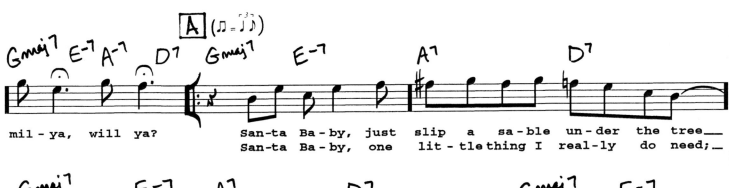

174

SILENT NIGHT

— FRANZ X. GRUBER/JOSEPH MOHR/JOHN F. YOUNG

Silver And Gold

—Johnny Marks

(Ballad)

Sil - ver and gold, sil - ver and gold, ev - 'ry-one wish - es for sil - ver and gold. How do you meas - ure its worth? Just by the pleas - ure it gives here on earth? Sil - ver and gold, sil - ver and gold mean so much more when I see sil - ver and gold dec-o - ra - tions on ev - 'ry Christ - mas tree. tree.

Silver Bells

178

(MED. SLOW)

—JAY LIVINGSTON/RAY EVANS

SING WE NOW OF CHRISTMAS

-TRADITIONAL FRENCH CAROL

SNOWFALL

Claude Thornhill / Ruth Thornhill

182

SOMEDAY AT CHRISTMAS

-Ronald N. Miller/Bryan Wells

(Med.)

184

THE STAR CAROL

(MED. SLOW)

—ALFRED BURT / WIHLA HUTSON

STILL, STILL, STILL

—Salzburg Melody, c. 1819 / Traditional Austrian Text

That Christmas Feeling

—Bennie Benjamin/George Weiss

How I love that Christ-mas feel - ing, how I treas-ure its friend-ly glow. See the way a stran-ger greets you just as though you'd met him Christ-mas-es a - go. Christ-mas helps you to re - mem - ber to do what oth - er folks hold dear. What a bless-ed place the world would be if we had that Christ-mas feel-ing all year.

Tennessee Christmas

—Amy Grant / Gary Chapman

192

(Rock Ballad) **THIS ONE'S FOR THE CHILDREN**

—Maurice Starr

There are some peo-ple__ liv-ing in__this world;__
Man-y peo-ple are hap - py__ and man - y peo-ple are sad.__

they have no food to eat,__ they have no place__ to go.__
Some peo-ple have man - y things_ that oth-ers can on - ly__ wish_they had.

But we all are God's chil-dren, we have to learn to love_ one an-oth - er.__
So, for the sake of the chil-dren, show_ them love's the on-ly way to go,__

Just re - mem - ber they_could be us,__ re-mem-ber we all_ are_broth - ers.__ }
'cause_they're our to-mor - row,__ and peo-ple, they've got_ to_ know.__ }

I'm not try - ing__ to dark - en up__ your day,__

but help oth - ers in need_ and show them there's a bet-ter__ way._

This one's for the chil - dren,__

the chil - dren of__ the world.__

TOYLAND

(MED. SLOW)

—Victor Herbert/Glen MacDonough

Toy - land, toy - land,
Child - hood's joy - land,

land, lit - tle girl and
land, mys - tic mer - ry

boy - land. While you dwell with -
joy - land. Once you pass its

in it, you are ev - er hap - py

then. bor - ders you can

nev - er re - turn a - gain.

Up On The Housetop

(MED. FAST)

-B.R. HANBY

Up   on the house - top___ rein - deer pause,
First comes the stock - ing of lit - tle Nell;
Next   comes the stock - ing of lit - tle Will;

out jumps good old   San - ta Claus;   down thru the chim - ney with
oh, dear San - ta,   fill it well.   Give her a dol - lie that
oh, just see what a   glo - rious fill. Here is a ham - mer and

lots of toys,   all for the lit - tle ones, Christ - mas joys.
laughs and cries, one that will o - pen and   shut her eyes.
lots of tacks,   al - so a ball and a   whip that cracks.

Ho, ho, ho!   Who would-n't go!   Ho, ho, ho!

Who would-n't go!___   Up on the house - top,   click, click, click.

Down thru the chim-ney with   good Saint Nick.   good Saint Nick.

196

(MED.) 'TWAS THE NIGHT BEFORE CHRISTMAS

-F. HENRI KLICKMAN / CLEMENT CLARKE MOORE

1. 'Twas the night be-fore Christ-mas, when all through the house, not a

2.-7. *See additional lyrics*

crea-ture was stir-ring, not e-ven a mouse. The

stock-ings were hung by the chim-ney with care in

hopes that Saint Nich-o-las soon would be there. The

chil-dren were nest-led all snug in their beds while

vis-ions of sug-ar plums danced through their heads. And

ma-ma in her 'ker-chief and I in my cap had just

set-tled our brains for a long win-ter's nap. 2. When___

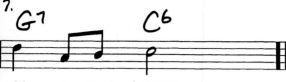

7.

all   a good night!"

Additional Lyrics

2. When out on the lawn there arose such a clatter,
   I sprang from my bed to see what was the matter.
   Away to the window I flew like a flash,
   Tore open the shutters and threw up the sash.
   The moon on the breast of the new-fallen snow
   Gave a lustre of midday to objects below;
   When what to my wondering eyes should appear
   But a miniature sleigh and eight tiny reindeer.

3. With a little old driver, so lively and quick,
   I knew in a moment it must be St. Nick.
   More rapid than eagles his coursers they came,
   And he whistled, and shouted, and called them by name:
   "Now, Dasher! Now, Dancer! Now, Prancer! Now, Vixen!
   On, Comet! On, Cupid! Oh, Donner and Blitzen!
   To the top of the porch, to the top of the wall!
   Now dash away, dash away, dash away all!"

4. As dry leaves that before the wild hurricane fly,
   When they meet with an obstacle, mount to the sky,
   So up to the house-top the coursers they flew,
   With the sleigh full of toys, and St. Nicholas, too.
   And then in a twinkling I heard on the roof
   The prancing and pawing of each little hoof.
   As I drew in my head and was turning around,
   Down the chimney St. Nicholas came with a bound.

5. He was dressed all in fur from his head to his foot,
   And his clothes were all tarnished with ashes and soot.
   A bundle of toys he had flung on his back,
   And he looked like a peddler just opening his pack.
   His eyes, how they twinkled! His dimples, how merry!
   His cheeks were like roses, his nose like a cherry.
   His droll little mouth was drawn up like a bow,
   And the beard of his chin was as white as the snow.

6. The stump of a pipe he held tight in his teeth,
   And the smoke, it encircled his head like a wreath.
   He had a broad face, and a round little belly
   That shook, when he laughed, like a bowl full of jelly.
   He was chubby and plump, a right jolly old elf,
   And I laughed when I saw him, in spite of myself.
   A wink of his eye, and a twist of his head,
   Soon gave me to know I had nothing to dread.

7. He spoke not a word, but went straight to his work
   And filled all the stockings, then turned with a jerk.
   And laying his finger aside of his nose,
   And giving a nod, up the chimney he rose.
   He sprang to his sleigh, to his team gave a whistle,
   And away they all flew like the down of a thistle.
   But I heard him exclaim, ere he drove out of sight,
   "Happy Christmas to all, and to all a good night!"

THE TWELVE DAYS OF CHRISTMAS

-TRADITIONAL ENGLISH CAROL

three French hens, two___ tur-tle doves, and a

par-tridge___ in a pear tree. 6. On the

sixth day of Christ-mas, my true love gave to me

REPEAT AS NEEDED (IGNORE 1st TIME)

six geese a-lay-ing, five gold-en

rings, four___ call-ing birds,

three French hens, two___ tur-tle doves, and a

1.-6. D.S.S. FOR VS. 7-12 7.

par-tridge___ in a pear tree. 7. On the tree.

7. On the seventh day of Christmas my true love gave to me
   seven swans a-swimming,…

8. … Eight maids a-milking,…

9. … Nine ladies dancing,…

10. … Ten lords a-leaping,…

11. … 'Leven pipers piping,…

12. … Twelve drummers drumming,…

200

We Need A Little Christmas

-Jerry Herman

(MED. FAST)

Haul out the hol - ly,_____ put up the
climb down the chim - ney,_____ turn on the

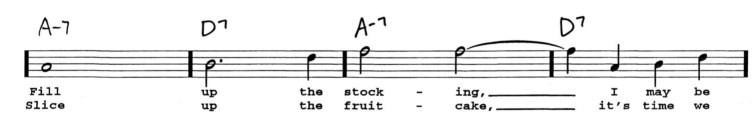

tree be - fore my spir - it falls____ a - gain.
bright - est string of lights I've ev - er seen.

Fill up the stock - ing,_____ I may be
Slice up the fruit - cake,_____ it's time we

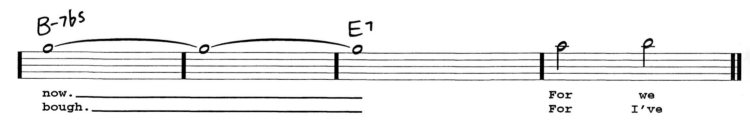

rush - ing things, but deck the halls____ a - gain
hung some tin - sel on that ev - er - green

now._____ For we
bough._____ For I've

need a lit - tle Christ - mas, right this ver - y min - ute,
grown a lit - tle lean - er, grown a lit - tle cold - er,
need a lit - tle mu - sic, need a lit - tle laugh - ter,

[SOLO ON ENTIRE FORM]

(MED.) WE THREE KINGS OF ORIENT ARE

-JOHN H. HOPKINS, JR.

E-7 ... **F#-7b5** **B7b9** **E-7**

We three kings of O - ri - ent are
Born a King on Beth - le - hem plain,

F#-7b5 **B7b9** **E-7**

bear - ing gifts, we tra - verse a - far,
gold I bring to crown Him a - gain:

D9 **Gmaj7** **Cmaj7**

field and foun - tain, moor and moun - tain,
King for - ev - er, ceas - ing nev - er,

F#-7b5 **B7#5** **B7** **E-7** **D7**

fol - low - ing yon - der star.
o - ver us all to reign.

G6 **E-7** **A-7** **D9** **G6**

star of won - der, star of night,

E-7 **A-7** **D9** **G6**

star with roy - al beau - ty bright.

E-7 **D9** **A-7** **D9**

West - ward lead - ing, still pro - ceed - ing,

G6 **E-7** **A-7** **D9** **1. G6** **2. G6**

guide us to thy per - fect light.   light.

(BRIGHT) We Wish You A Merry Christmas

—Traditional English Folksong

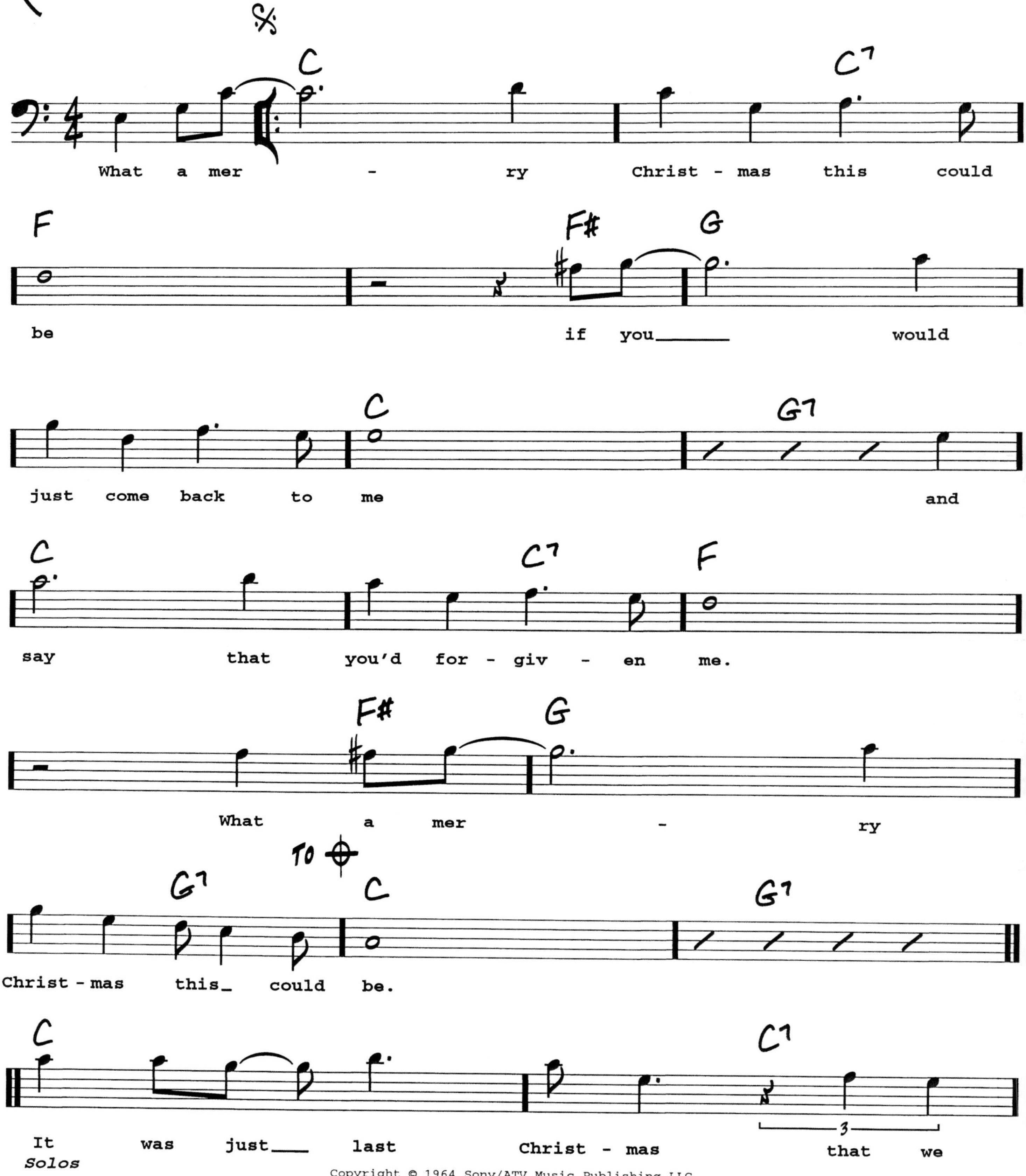

What a Merry Christmas This Could Be

(Country Swing)

—Hank Cochran/Harlan Howard

C
C7
What a mer - ry Christ - mas this could
F
F#
G
be if you___ would
C
G7
just come back to me and
C
C7
F
say that you'd for - giv - en me.
F#
G
What a mer - ry
TO
G7
C
G7
Christ - mas this_ could be.
C
C7
It was just___ last Christ - mas that we
Solos
3

(Med.) WHILE SHEPHERDS WATCHED THEIR FLOCKS

—George Frideric Handel/Nahum Tate

Additional Lyrics

3."To you, in David's town this day,
Is born of David's line
The Savior who is Christ the Lord,
And this shall be the sign,
And this shall be the sign:

4."The heav'nly Babe you there shall find
To human view displayed,
All meanly wrapped in swathing bands
And in a manger laid,
And in a manger laid.

5."All glory be to God on high,
And to the earth be peace.
Good will henceforth from heav'n to men
Begin and never cease,
Begin and never cease."